MW00997961

Mastering Modes for Guitar

An easy to follow guide to learning the major scale and its modes

By Glen Ross

ISBN: 9781983152320
Imprint: Independently published

Forward

I have been teaching guitar for many (MANY) years now, and when it comes to "scales and modes", it's always been a topic of confusion.

In my opinion, there are two sides to the mystery of this coin: 1. How to see (and play) them on the guitar 2. Understanding the application for actually using them in your playing

...and if you know anything about my style of teaching, it's similar to my dad's best childhood story;

"I didn't know how to swim, so my best friend took me to the bridge near my house, and threw me in the lake...I learned how to swim".

I never knew if this story was true, and my dad has since passed away, but I always CHOSE for it to be true, because it's a platform on which I tend to live my life (and my guitar playing)...

Play NOW and figure it all out later.

Why do I say this? Because all too many times, I encounter guitar players who are waiting for the perfect answer, or they think they need to study theory for 8 years before they can play with other musicians, or simply don't realize there are many different ways to "approach" a concept, and the key is this:

Play NOW and fix things that need to be fixed as you go. Learn the "hows and the whys" but learn them after you have experienced rocking out to an AC/DC tune thru an EXTREMELY LOUD tube amplifier with your friends 😵

So why am I telling you this?

Because Glen Ross has got a cool little book here for you that does just that: it gets you playing (and seeing) scales on the guitar (in a very creative and simple manner, by the way), and THEN it tells you how to apply this information in a theoretical sense.

When it comes to guitar playing, I have always approached it from 3 points of view:

1. Know very little but have fun on the journey (until you are ready for another "level")

2. Know too much and forget how to have fun

3. Know what is the "right amount" for YOU and your guitar journey, and gain power, confidence and clarity along the way.

For me, that's what this book does. Even if you only studied the first part and learned how to "see" the guitar for your brand of soloing and musical approach, you have already won.

But if you decide to dive further to reach that next level, the second half of the book does that, and does it very well.

I have been playing my entire life, and there isn't a day that goes by that I am not learning or reinforcing something about my playing in some capacity, and I am being quite honest when I tell you I found Glen's approach refreshing.

Just don't go too fast, slow down and enjoy the journey, and don't forget to jump into the lake once in a while.

Steve

www.stevestineofficial.com

Introduction

Playing the guitar is a fun and rewarding life-long journey of discovery. It seems that the more you study the more there is to learn. One of the major stumbling blocks for many guitarists is learning the major scale and especially the modes. It can be confusing.

If you have never attempted to learn the modes, or are having trouble understanding them, this is the book for you. My method incorporates all three learning styles seeing, hearing and doing. No, there are not sound files involved. You will hear yourself playing the scales and modes as you do what the text explains.

This book is the product of my journey learning the modes. I tried reading books and working with guitar teachers but none of them could explain the modes in simple plain English. That is why I set out to learn them on my own. This book is the result of my efforts.

Over the years, I have taught this method to guitarist of many levels with great results. My goal with this book was to create the ultimate resource for learning the major scale and its modes. All modesty aside, I believe I have achieved my goal by creating a step by step method to mastering the modes. It is my sincere hope that once you have finished the book you agree with me.

I suggest you read the book at least twice. In the first reading, remember that you don't have to master each step or exercise before moving on. You will notice there is no table of contents as the book is intended to be read cover to cover. Each section builds upon the previous section. The second reading is to help fill in any gaps and put the earlier sections into perspective once you understand the big picture.

After you have read the book, please leave a review on amazon.com to help other guitarists make an informed choice when looking for a resource to learn the modes. While five stars would be nice, I am looking for honest feedback on your experience with the book.

You can check out some of my music on at:
https://www.reverbnation.com/glenross

Seven Patterns to Heaven

Like many guitar players I spent many years playing in bands with no knowledge of the major scale and its modes. I learned songs by ear memorizing them note for note. I had success doing this for many years with no idea that I was doing it the hard way. That all changed when I joined an original band as their lead guitarist. I no longer had the luxury of simply imitating what someone else had played. It was now my job to develop original leads and riffs.

After doing some research and talking to other guitarists, I realized that I needed to learn the modes of the major scale. I read many books and went to a few teachers, but it just didn't click. You may be in the same or a similar position. With no one able to describe how the modes worked in a simple, understandable form I set out to learn them on my own. I spent years studying and analyzing guitar theory on my own. Those years of discovery are what brought me to write this book. My goal is to save you the time and frustration that I experienced in my journey.

One of my first discoveries was the seven patterns that make up all the major scale and its modes. With these patterns, you can play any mode in any key without worrying about what notes you are playing. That is not to say that knowing the notes on the fretboard and knowing what notes are in each mode are not important to a complete understanding of them, and we will be looking at that before and as you learn the notes involved.

There is considerable memorization involved but it's not nearly as hard as the teachers I worked with made it sound. The key is learning the information in the right order. That said, please read the book from front to back instead of jumping ahead. Sure, some of the information may seem remedial. If you already know what I'm talking about, you are ahead of the game that much. I am assuming that you know basic chords and can find notes on the fretboard.

I'll begin with some terms you will need to know to understand how to use the seven patterns. Then we'll look at the patterns one by one followed by a description about how to put them together in a useful way.

Things to Know

Fret – the vertical metal bars that run down the guitar's neck.

Step – a span of two frets.

Interval – the space between two notes.

Half-step – a span of one fret.

Root – the central tone for a chord, scale or mode.

Finger Numbering

On your right hand the fingers are numbered 1 through 4. 1 is your index finger, 2 is your middle finger, 3 is the ring finger and 4 is your pinky.

The Fretboard

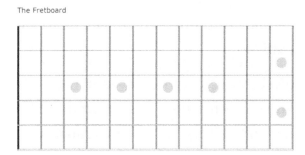

The Fretboard

The fretboard diagrams will be on 12 fret fretboard as seen above. The Bottom of the diagram is the low E string. The top of the diagram is the high E string. From bottom to top the strings are E, A, D, G, B and E. This is standard for guitar texts.

Pattern 1

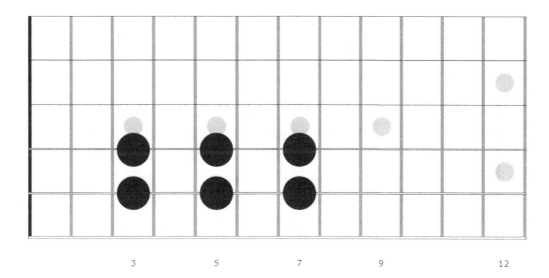

Pattern one is the natural major scale known as the Ionian mode.   It sounds good over a major chord as well as a major 7th chord. It is major because the third note is two steps above the root (first note in this case). It is formed by starting at the root note. The second note is one step up and the third is one step above the second. The rest of the pattern is the same intervals one string down.

While this is not a book on technique, I am going to suggest how to play the patterns. For the Ionian pattern, place your thumb behind the fret one step above the starting note. In the case of the example that would be behind the 4th fret. The first note is played with your 1st finger, the second note with your 3rd and the third note with your 4th finger.

Note that you must count the root as number one when looking for the third.

It is important to note that this pattern can be played anywhere on the fretboard. The key you are playing in is determined by the root note (the note to the bottom right of the diagram or top right on the fretboard).

There, of course, is an exception to the rule and that is when you start the pattern on the G string. Due to the tuning of the B string the second half of the pattern needs shifted by a half-step or one fret. You can see that in the diagram below. Note that you may wish to shift your thumb up one step to facilitate the stretch of your pinky.

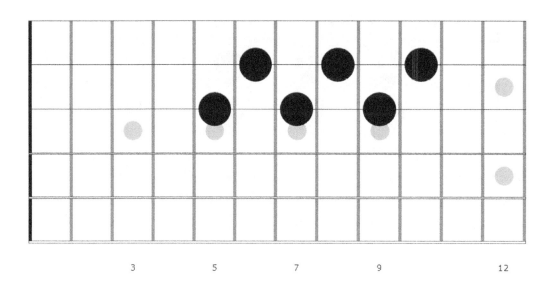

Both patterns shown above are in the key of C major (Ionian), but you can start on any note on the fretboard depending on which key you wish to play. To play in the key of G, you would start on the third fret of the low E string or example.

Memorize pattern one and don't forget to tell yourself that you are playing pattern one as that will be vital when we start putting the patterns together later in the book.

Pattern 2

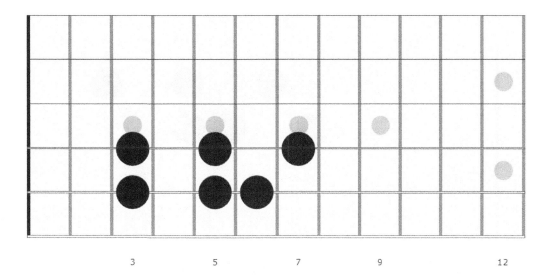

Pattern 2 is a minor scale and is referred to as the Dorian mode. It is minor because the third note is only a step and a half above the root meaning it will sound good over a minor chord, Cm in this example. The third note will always determine whether a mode is major or minor. Major modes have the third two steps above the root while minor modes have the third note a step and a half above the root.

The second pattern is formed by starting at the root. The second note is a step above the root and the third is a half-step above the second. The string below is the note below the root followed by two full steps.

As with pattern one, and all the patterns for that matter, pattern two can be started anywhere on the fretboard with the first note determining the key you are playing. For example, if you start on the top, or sixth, string third fret you are playing a G Dorian as opposed to a C Dorian as pictured in the diagram. It is important to keep this in mind.

The same exception exists for patterns played on the G and B strings due to tuning. Remember to slide your thumb up a step to facilitate the pinky stretch.

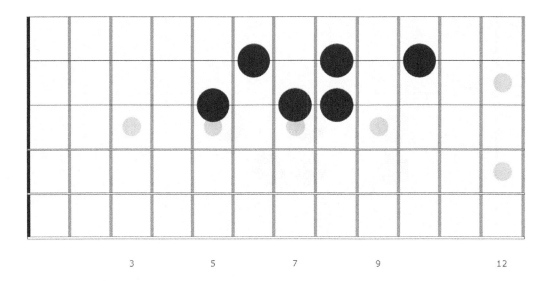

Memorize pattern two and work on visualizing where the notes are just as you did in pattern one. Be sure to tell yourself that you are playing pattern two as you do this. Trust me it will be important later.

Take a few minutes to reread the sections for pattern one and pattern two noting the similarities between them such as the portability as well as the differences such as one is major and two is minor.

Pattern 3

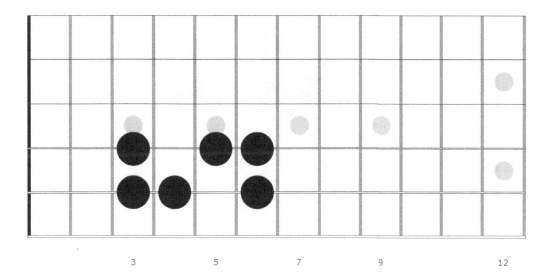

Look at pattern three and notice that like pattern two it is minor due to the third note being only a step and a half above the root. That means, like pattern two, it sounds good over a minor chord. In this case it would be Cm.

Pattern three is the Phrygian mode. It is formed by staring at the root followed by a half step then a full stip. The next string down is the opposite: a full step followed by a half step.

Like the other two patterns, pattern three can be played anywhere on the fretboard depending on what note you want to use as the root note. The exception for the G and B strings still exists as you will see on the following figure.

Memorize pattern two as you did with the previous two patterns remembering to tell yourself that you are playing pattern three. Try to visualize where the notes are as you don't have to play them in any particular order. The patterns simply show which notes can be played in the scale.

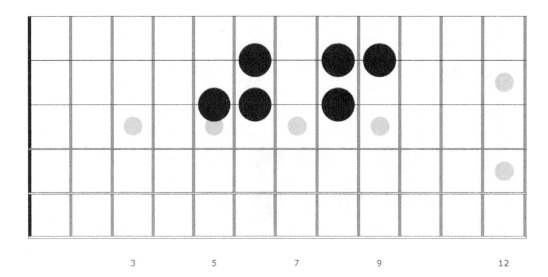

If you have a friend that plays or the ability to record yourself, this would be a good time to play the patterns over a droning chord. The diagrams are all in the key of C so pattern one sounds good over a C major and patterns two and three sound good over a C minor.

I can't emphasize enough how important it is to visualize the patterns in your mind as you play them. As we progress through the method, you will understand why.

You will notice some notes sound better against the chord while others create a sense of dissonance. Some notes are stronger than others and we'll look at the why and wherefores of that later in the book. For now, enjoy the sounds you are able to create as you play the notes in the pattern against the chord.

If you don't have a partner or the ability to record, play the chord then notes from the pattern while the sound of the chord is fresh in your mind.

Pattern 4

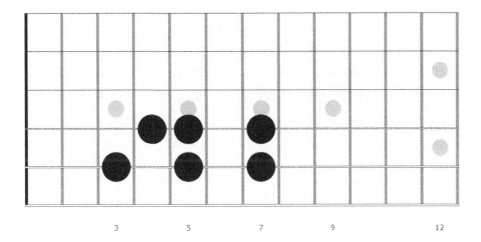

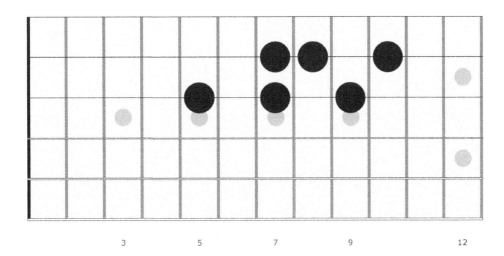

You will notice that I put both figures for pattern four on one page. As with all the patterns, the G, B string exception exists. Note that on the G and B string example we shift up two frets: one for the tuning difference and the second because the second-string pattern begins with a half-step. This will be a rule from now on. If a pattern starts with a half-step, you shift up a half-step when you play it. Don't forget to shift your thumb also.

Pattern four is a major pattern due to the third note being two steps above the root and is called the Lydian Mode. It sounds good over a major chord. Memorize pattern four remembering to tell yourself that you are playing pattern four and visualizing the pattern as you go. As with all the patterns practice playing the notes in different orders as you visualize the pattern.

As you practice, be sure to refresh yourself on the previous patterns also. To effectively use this method, they need to become second nature and they will with time.

Pattern 5

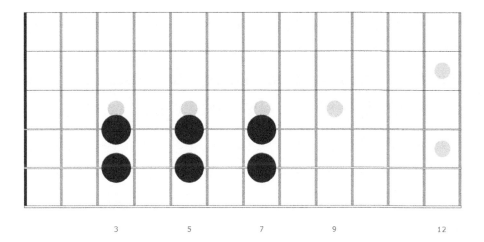

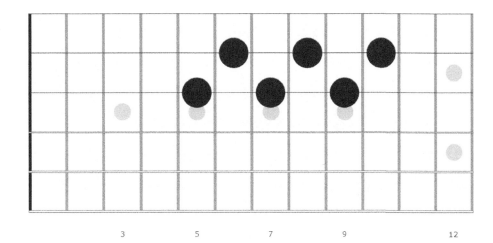

The first thing you will notice about pattern five is that it is identical to pattern one. While this is true, keep in mind that like identical twins, they are two separate entities. This will become clear soon when we start putting the patterns together.

Pattern five is a major mode due to its third note being two steps above the root. It is called the Mixolydian mode and sounds good over a major chord, especially over the 7th chord.

Memorize and visualize pattern five as you did the others. Do not forget to tell yourself that you are playing pattern five, not pattern one.

Pattern 6

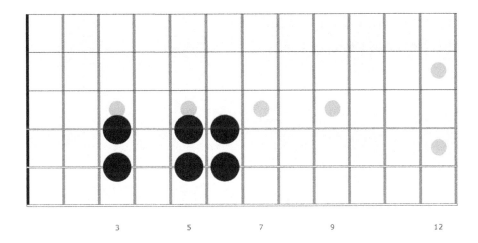

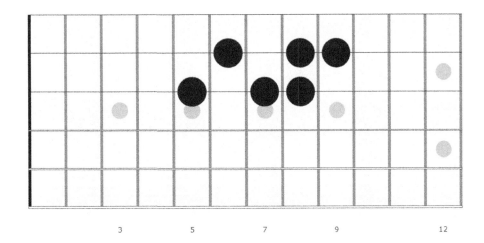

Pattern six is the natural minor mode known as the Aeolian mode. You will notice it is minor due to the third note. It sounds good over a minor chord.

There is not much more to say about this pattern except to memorize and visualize it as you did the previous patterns telling yourself that you are playing pattern six.

I know the patterns are a lot to remember and learn but believe me that it will be worth it very soon. As we put things together you will be able to play any mode in any key all over the fretboard with ease.

Pattern 7

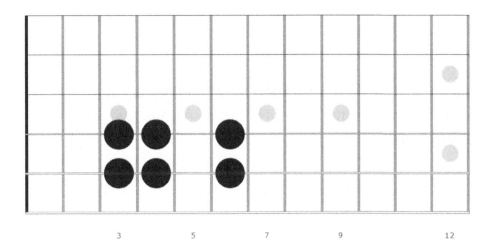

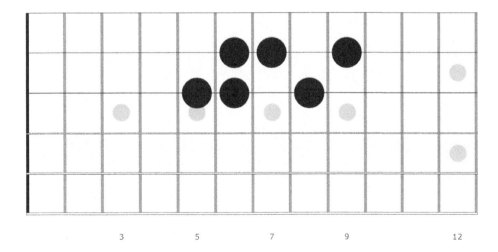

Pattern seven is the Locrian Mode and it is virtually useless as a mode. It sounds good, relatively speaking, over a diminished chord with a flatted fifth. Despite its uselessness as a mode, it is as important as the rest as a pattern. It is a minor mode due to the third note being a step and a half above the root.

Learn, memorize and visualize this pattern like you did the previous six taking heart in knowing this is the last one you have to memorize. The next step in our journey is to put the patterns together into usable modes.

Before moving on in this book, please make sure that you know all the patterns by heart as well as which number they are. The mode names are not as important at this time. They will be reinforced as we progress.

Putting It All Together Horizontally

Now that you know all seven patterns we can begin to put them together into something useful. First, we will look at the horizontal direction then we'll tackle the vertical.

...1, 2, 3, 4, 5, 6, 7, 1, 2 ,3, 4, 5, 6, 7, 1...

Notice in the number series above, it counts from one to seven and then repeats like a circle. This is how the patterns fit together. One is always followed by two, two by three etcetera. It is important to note that one is preceded by seven and one comes after seven. All the patterns are used in each mode.

Look at the figures on the next pages to see how the patterns fit together horizontally. You will see that they overlap. One pattern is in black, the next pattern is in gray. The notes that are black and gray are shared between the two patterns.

Using the figures, you can find the patterns all the way up, or down, the neck. Which pattern you start with determines the mode you are playing. Where you start (the root note) will determine which key you are in.

All the patterns start on the G note on the E string, so they will be a mode of G.

Pattern 1 & 2 are in the G Ionian mode.

Pattern 2 & 3 are in the G Dorian mode.

Pattern 3 & 4 are in the G Phrygian mode.

Pattern 4 & 5 are in the G Lydian mode.

Pattern 5 & 6 are in the G Mixolydian mode.

Pattern 7 & 1 are in the G Locrian mode.

If the previous breakdown does not make sense to you, I recommend you reread the book from the beginning until the light comes on. It is important that you understand each of the statements.

Practice the horizontal extensions until you are comfortable with them before moving on to the next section.

1 & 2

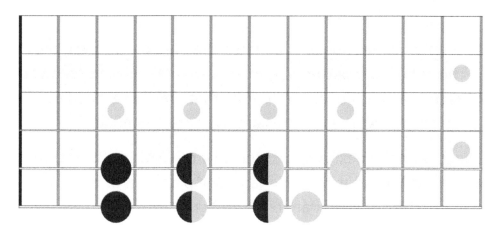

2 & 3

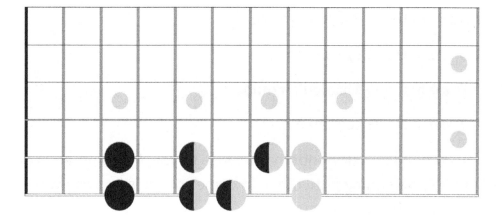

3 & 4

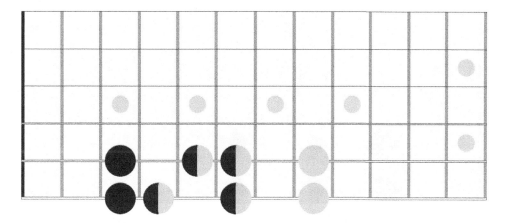

4 & 5

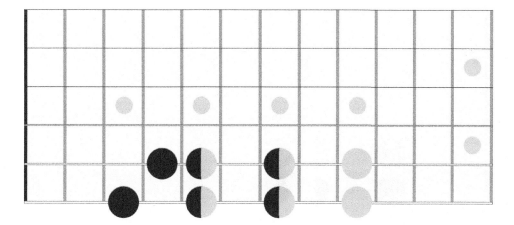

5 & 6

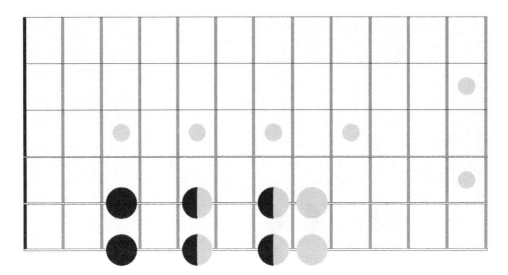

6 & 7

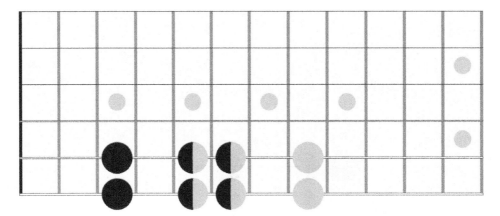

7 & 1

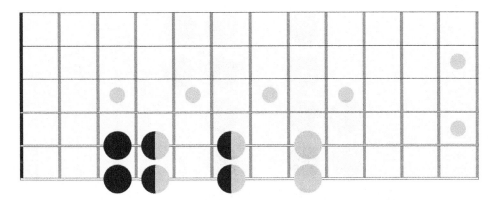

Remember that you can play these patterns starting anywhere on the fretboard. If you start the pattern on the G string, don't forget to shift the second half up one fret.

Putting It All Together Vertically

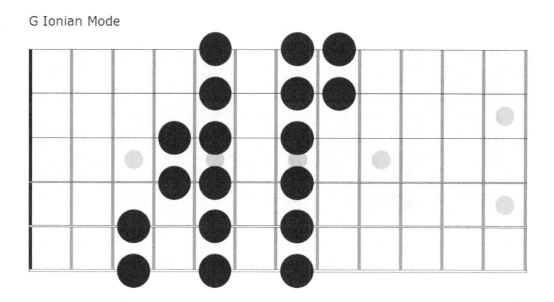

G Ionian Mode

In the figure above is the G Ionian mode. It is G Ionian because we are starting with pattern one on the G note on the low E string. Since we are going down the fretboard, we subtract one to get the next pattern. Below pattern one therefore will be pattern seven. Below pattern seven is pattern six.

Notice how pattern six is shifted up one fret to accommodate the G to B string tuning.

Going from the bottom to the top, you simply add one to find the pattern. Starting from pattern six you get pattern seven. Then the top pattern is one more than seven, or one.

G Dorian Mode

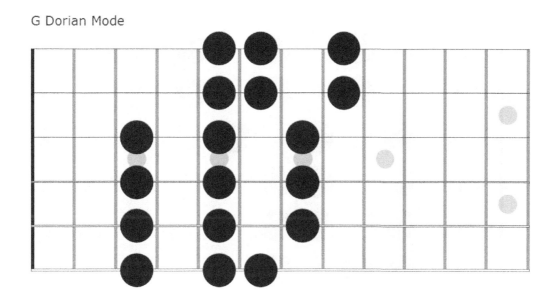

The figure above shows the G Dorian mode since we are starting with pattern two on the G note of the low E string. Remember that you can start on any note on the fretboard to change the key. For example, if I started on the eighth fret I would be playing C Dorian.

Starting with pattern two we have pattern one just below it. Pattern seven is below pattern one since seven is one less than one.

Notice the full step shift on the B string: one fret for tuning and the other because the pattern starts with a half-step.

Practice the Dorian mode, as well as the other modes, in both directions. Remember that you don't have to play the notes in any order. By adding variety, you will discover more interesting melodies.

G Phrygian Mode

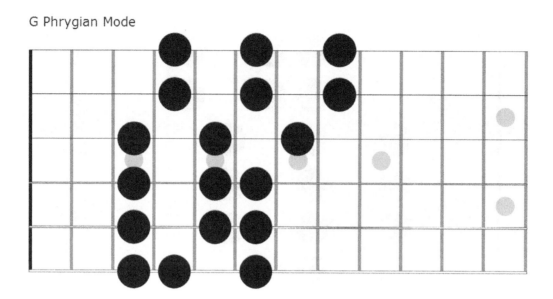

The above figure shows the G Phrygian mode. Notice how it starts with pattern three with the first note on the G on the low E string. Below pattern three on the fretboard we have pattern two followed by pattern one. Pattern one has been shifted up one fret because of tuning.

As you practice this mode, and the others, be sure to keep track of which pattern you are playing and what comes before and after each one.

By now, you are probably noticing other patterns within the mode. Starting on the C on the A string you can see C Aonian. Starting with the F on the D string you can see F Dorian. The mode you are playing depends on what you choose as the root. We will look at this more when we start looking at the actual notes you are playing. It's no wonder that our minds get confused when discussing scales and modes. For now, focus on the mechanics of playing the patterns. By the time you finish this book, hopefully the confusion will be cleared up.

G Lydian Mode

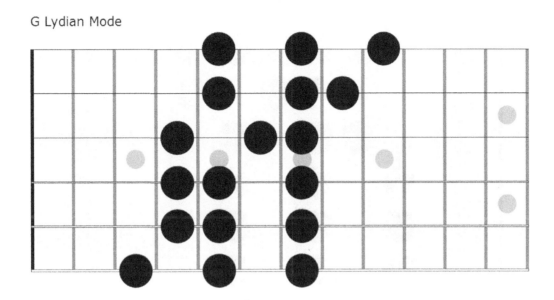

The figure above shows the G Lydian mode. Notice how it starts with pattern four on the G on the low E string. Below pattern four is pattern three with pattern two, shifted a half-step of course, below it.

Granted, it seems I am repeating myself simply substituting different numbers, but it is important to me to make sure you see the patterns as they fit together. If you know what I am going to say before I say it, then you are ahead of the game. Please, bear with me as we only have three more to go.

By now, I hope these patterns have become part of your normal practice routine. If not, I suggest you add them. Through experience I have found that twenty minutes is a good amount of time to practice before taking a break. Your mind starts to wander if you study one thing for much longer. Play some licks, your favorite song or just take a short break between twenty-minute stints practicing anything. Your mind will absorb what you are learning much easier that way.

G Mixolydian Mode

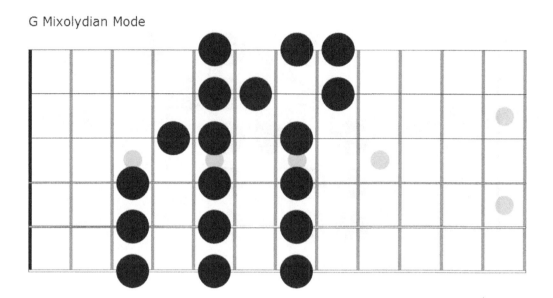

This is the G Mixolydian mode. It is built by starting with pattern five on the G of the low E string. Below pattern five is pattern four with pattern three, shifted, below it.

Learn this mode, as with the other modes, forward and backward, visualizing where the notes are on the fretboard. The Mixolydian mode sounds great over the dominant seventh chord (G7 in this case).

The Mixolydian mode is one of the more common modes in rock, country and popular music. It is less jazzy than the Ionian mode and less free sounding than the Lydian mode.

By now as you practice these modes, you are likely to hear the different moods each of the modes create.

G Aeolian Mode

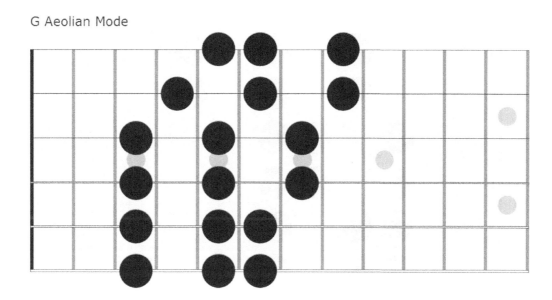

The figure above shows the G Aeolian mode. Pattern six starts on the G on the low E string. Below is pattern five with the shifted pattern four below it.

The Aeolian mode is also known as the natural minor. We will look at the relationship between the major and the natural minor later in this book. Suffice it to say that the major (Ionian) mode and its natural minor (Aeolian) mode contain the same notes.

We are almost through the modes vertically and by now you hopefully will be enjoying the music you are able to make with them. Don't forget to practice all of them forward, backward and in different orders as you play them against a droning chord progression. Remember to look at the third note to determine if the mode is major (two full steps from the root to the third) or minor (a step and a half between the root and the third).

G Locrian Mode

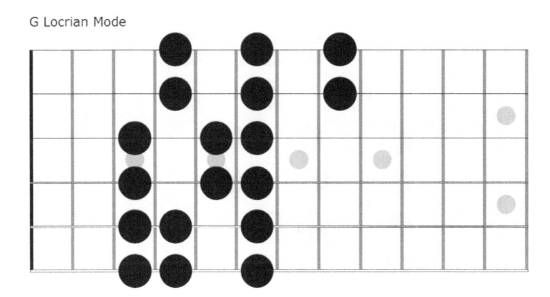

This Locrian mode is shown in the figure above. It is formed by playing pattern seven starting on the G on the low E string. Below pattern seven is pattern six followed by pattern five (shifted of course due to tuning).

Practice this mode even though it is hard to play over any chord. In this case it plays over Gdim*b*5. It is as important as all the other modes acting as a bridge between the Aeolian and Ionian modes. If that statement doesn't make sense, refer to the diagram for the Ionian mode and notice how pattern seven (Locrian) comes between pattern one (Ionian) and pattern six (Aeolian).

At this point, you should be able, with some thinking, to combine the patterns both horizontally and vertically into useable scales. The next step is to look at them joined in a combination of horizontally and vertically. We are now going to look at them diagonally.

Putting It Together Diagonally

By combining vertical and horizontal patterns you can move across the fretboard in a diagonal direction. On the next page I show just one of the possibilities in all seven modes.

In the Ionian example, I started with pattern one then added the first note of pattern seven. After the first note of pattern seven, I shift up one half-step with my index finger. This note is the second note of pattern seven, but I use it as the first note of pattern one again. Below the second pattern one, I play the first note of pattern seven again. Notice how it is shifted up another fret due to tuning. I then shift up one half-step and repeat pattern one.

Each of the next six examples follow the same procedure but with the corresponding pattern at the start: pattern two for Dorian, pattern three for Phrygian etcetera. Study the figures and pick out the patterns. This is where visualizing the patterns comes in very handy.

It takes a while to get proficient at putting the patterns together and visualizing where the notes are. Don't be discouraged if you must stop and think about it as you learn and practice them. Any worthwhile skill takes work and time. The rewards are well worth the effort. If necessary, go back in the book and work on earlier sections until you are proficient at visualizing and playing the patterns in those sections then try the more complex concepts again.

Whether you are having trouble applying the patterns or you are comfortable doing it, move forward in the book as it is about to change focus to the actual notes and intervals involved in the patterns. Either way, continue to practice the patterns as you progress through the book.

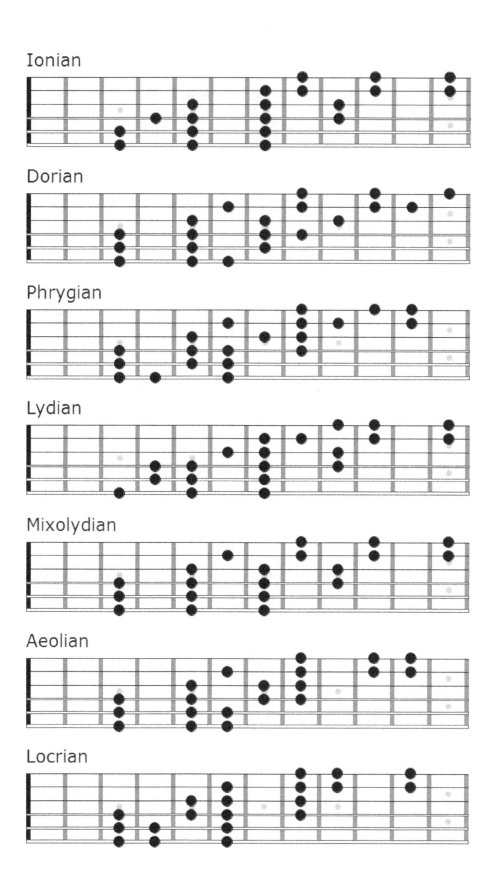

Intervals

Intervals

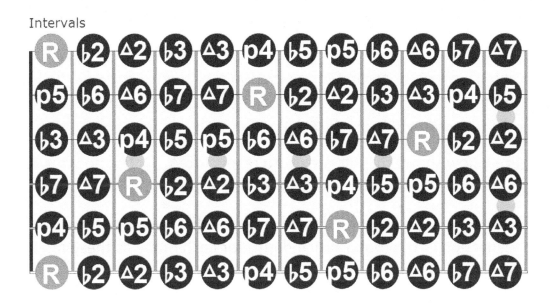

The diagram above shows all the intervals on the first twelve frets with respect to the F note. Notice that all the F notes have a white R in the center. The R stands for root and it is the most compatible (consonant) note with any F chord''

The fourth and fifth are marked with a 'p'. The 'p' stands for perfect. The perfect intervals do not have both a major and minor equivalent. The fourth can be augmented (#4) or the fifth can be diminished (b5).

The fifth interval is the second strongest, or compatible, note next to the root. You should note the location of the fifth to the root as it never changes. It is always one string up or one string down and two frets up from the root.

The fourth is always one string down or one string up and two frets back. The only exception is between the G and B string due to tuning; here the notes on the B string are shifted up one fret.

The second, third, sixth and seventh all have major and minor intervals. The most important out of this group is the major and minor thirds.

The third in a scale always determines whether a chord, or scale, is major or minor. Except for the G and B string where everything is shifted up one fret, the major third interval is always one string down and one fret lower. The minor third is one string down and two frets lower.

Unless you have a photographic memory, don't try to memorize all the intervals. Focus on the ones I've identified: the root, the thirds, the fourth and the fifth. The rest of the intervals can be located using these as a reference.

The figure below shows the intervals with respect to A. Notice how the relative position of the intervals with respect to the roots does not change.

On the following page, I've added the intervals to the diagrams for each mode. Note the location of the root, third and fifth for each mode as these are the strongest notes in the mode.

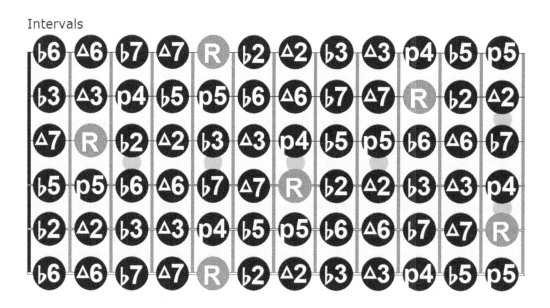

Intervals

G Ionian Mode

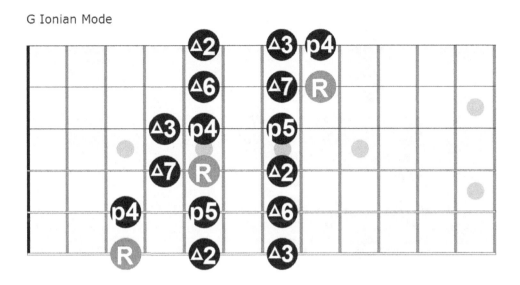

G Dorian Mode

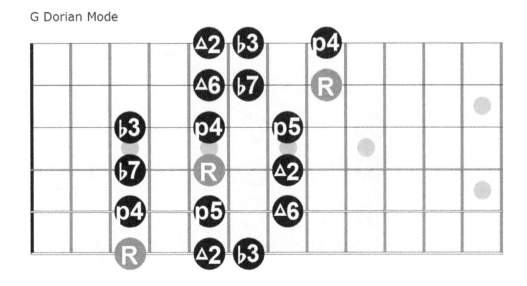

Mastering the Modes for Guitar

G Phrygian Mode

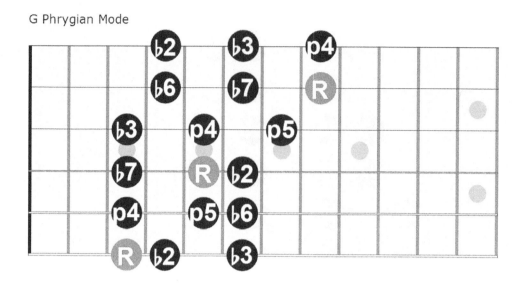

G Lydian Mode

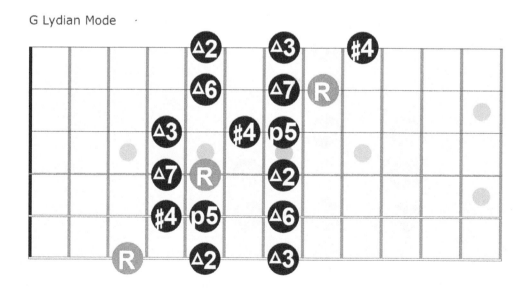

G Mixolydian Mode

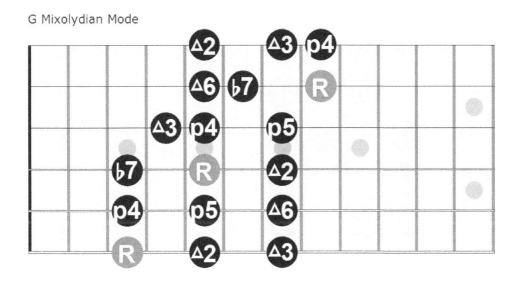

G Aeolian Mode

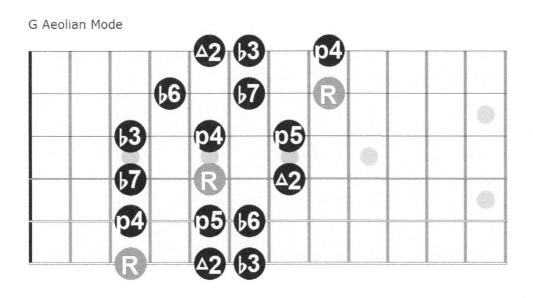

G Locrian Mode

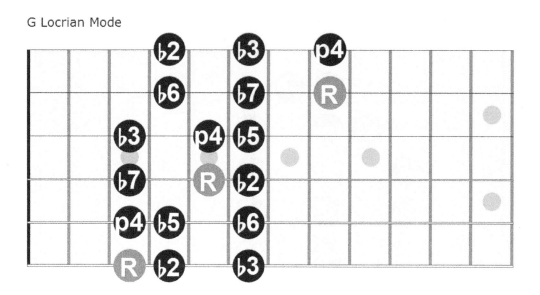

From root to root is the interval called an octave. The octave means it is the eighth note of the scale. Notice every interval from the root has a corresponding octave. Also notice in the diagrams above they are showing two octaves as they show the intervals from root to root twice.

The Circle of Fifths

It is now time to put the note names into the patterns. Before we do this, we should learn the circle of fifths. The best way to learn the circle of fifths is to learn how to draw it. As you draw it over and over, you will be able to memorize the information the circle of fifths provides.

Many years ago, a guitar instructor told me that the key to the circle of fifths is two mnemonics.

Father **C**harles **G**oes **D**own **A**nd **E**nds **B**attle

Battle **E**nds **A**nd **D**own **G**oes **C**harles' **F**ather

Memorize both phrases as they will be vital to your understanding of the circle of fifths. Notice that the second mnemonic is just the first mnemonic reversed. The first letter of each word represents a musical note. The notes are not in alphabetical order like they are on the fretboard, they are ordered by fifths in the first mnemonic and by fourths in the second. There will be more about this shortly.

As I stated, the notes on the fretboard are in alphabetical order:

...A, B, C, D, E, F, G, A, B, C, D, E, F, G, A, B, C, D, E, F, G...

Between most of the notes are the accidental notes, sharps and flats, the exception being between B and C and E and F.

...A, A#/Bb, B, C, C#/Db, D, D#/Eb, E, F, F#/Gb, G, G#/Ab, A, A#/Bb, B, C...

There are twelve notes to an octave (the interval between roots) that simply repeat.

If you look at the musical alphabet above ignoring the accidentals, counting from F (**F**ather) as one, C (**C**harles) is the fifth. The fifth of C is G, the fifth of G is D, the fifth of D is A, the fifth of A is E and the fifth of E is B. The Fifth of B is F# whose fifth is C# and so on. Notice the correspondence between this order and the first mnemonic.

The second mnemonic follows a similar pattern except is denotes the fourth note. Starting at B (**B**attle), the fourth would be E. The fourth of E (**E**nds) is A and so on. This explains the second mnemonic.

The first mnemonic denotes the fifths and the second denotes the fourths.

It is time to learn how to draw the circle of fifths. Granted, it would be easier to simply purchase, or download, a copy of the circle of fifths but you won't walk away with as deep an understanding as you will by learning to draw it for yourself.

To begin, draw a circle. Divide the circle into 12 equal parts like a clock. I start with the top and bottom (12:00 and 6:00). Perpendicular lines at 9:00 and 3:00. Then draw two equally spaced perpendicular lines between the lines you've drawn.

Once this is done, Write C above the 12:00 line and F# below the 6:00 line.

Next fill in the notes starting with F at 11:00, G at 1:00, D at 2:00, A at 3:00, E at 4:00 and B at 5:00. Notice how this follows the first mnemonic.

Next, I fill in from 10:00 to 7:00 with the word BEAD. All four of these are flat notes so at 10:00 I have Bb, 9:00 has Eb, 8:00 has Ab and 7:00 has Db.

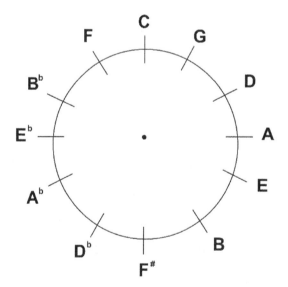

The next step is to fill in the relative minors inside the circle. Starting at 8:00 write Fm inside the circle across from Ab. This means that Fm is the relative minor for Ab. Using the first mnemonic fill in from 9:00 to 2:00.

9:00 is Cm, 10:00 is Gm, 11:00 is Dm, 12:00 is Dm, 1:00 is Em and 2:00 is Bm. Fill in the rest of the relative minors with F#m at 3:00, Dbm at 4:00, Abm at 5:00, Ebm at 6:00 and Bbm at 7:00.

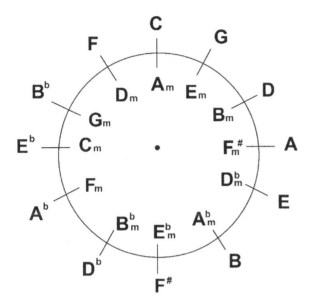

Now it is time to finish the right side of the circle. The key of C has no flats or sharps, so we do nothing for C.

Moving clockwise, G has one sharp and it happens to be F#. this means that the F in the G major scale is replaced by F#. Note that F corresponds to the word **F**ather in the first mnemonic (see the figure).

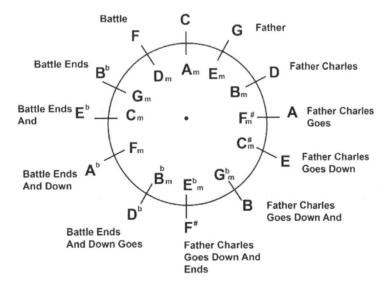

Next moving clockwise is D. D has two sharps, F# and C# corresponding to **F**ather **C**harles in the first mnemonic. This is followed by A which has three sharps: F#, C# and G# according to the firsts mnemonic. E is next with four sharps: F#, C#, G# and D#. B has five sharps: F#, C#, G#, D# and A#. Finally, F# has 6 sharps: F#, C#, G#, D#, A# and E#.

While the right side of the circle has sharp notes, the left side will have flat notes.

Now it's time to fill in the left side of the circle. Here we use the second mnemonic. At 11:00, F has one flat and it is Bb corresponding to **B**attle. Moving counter-clockwise, Bb has two flats: Bb and Eb corresponding to **B**attle **E**nds. Eb has three flats: Bb, Eb and Ab. Ab has four flats: Bb, Eb, Ab and Db. Lastly, Db has five flats: Bb, Eb, Ab, Db and Gb.

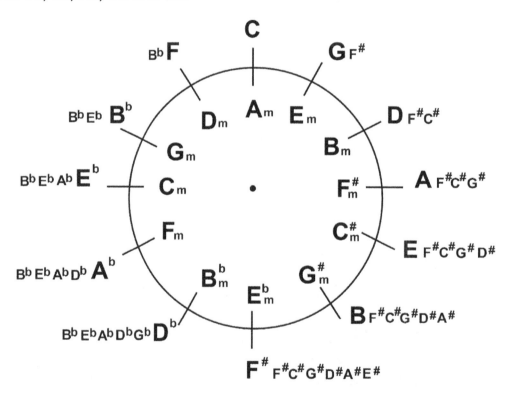

Now the circle of fifths is complete. Draw it until you no longer need the instructions to do so. By that time, you likely will have it memorized to the point where you can determine the sharps and flats in any key.

See the chart below to see a summary of the circle of fifths information.

Sharps

	F#	C#	G#	D#	A#	E#	B#
C							
G	X						
D	X	X					
A	X	X	X				
E	X	X	X	X			
B	X	X	X	X	X		
F#	X	X	X	X	X	X	
C#	X	X	X	X	X	X	X

Flats

	Bb	Eb	Ab	Db	Gb	Cb	Fb
C							
F	X						
Bb	X	X					
Eb	X	X	X				
Ab	X	X	X	X			
Db	X	X	X	X	X		
Gb	X	X	X	X	X	X	
Cb	X	X	X	X	X	X	X

The C major key

The key of C major has no accidentals. The notes in the C Ionian scale are: C, D, E, F, G, A, B and back to C to start a new octave. To play the C Ionian scale, you start on any C note on the fretboard and begin with pattern one. See the figure for the C Ionian scale on the following pages to see all the notes in the scale on the first twelve frets.

The strongest notes against a C chord will be the first (C) third (E) and fifth (G) notes of the scale. These three notes are known as the C triad. A C chord anywhere on the fretboard is comprised of these three notes.

The C Ionian mode can be played over other forms of the C major chord. Any note in the scale can be added to the C major chord to create other chords.

The Cmaj7 is formed by adding the major seventh note (B) to the chord. When played across a Cmaj7 the seventh note also becomes a strong note to focus he on. The C Ionian does not work well with a C7 because the major 7th interval will clash with the minor seventh (dominant seventh) in the C7 chord.

The C6 chord adds the sixth note (A) to the chord making the A a strong note against the chord.

A C9 chord adds the ninth note (D which is the same as the second note) to the chord. Across a C9 chord, the D note becomes a strong note.

If you start the scale on the second note, D, you are playing the D Dorian mode. The notes in the D Dorian mode are D, E, F, G, A, B, C then back to D to start a new octave. When playing the D Dorian mode, you start on any D on the fretboard and play pattern two (see figure for the D Dorian mode). Since the third note (F) is a minor third the D Dorian mode is played over a Dm chord

The strongest notes against a Dm chord with be the first (D), third (F) and fifth (A) of the Dorian mode. These notes form the Dm triad.

The D Dorian mode can be played over any form of the Dm chord.

The Dm7 is formed by adding the seventh note (C). Since the C is a flat seventh, it is called a dominant seventh. When playing the D Dorian over a Dm7 chord, the C becomes a strong note.

A Dm6 chord adds the sixth note (B) making it a strong note against the Dm6 chord, and a Dm9 adds the ninth note (E) making it a strong note against the Dm9 chord.

The Phrygian mode of the C major scale is created by starting on the third note (E) anywhere on the fretboard and playing the third pattern. The notes for the E Phrygian mode are E, F, G, A, B, C, D and back to E, the octave. The third note (G) is a flat third making the Phrygian mode a minor mode, so it is played over an Em.

To play the E Phrygian mode start pattern three on any E note on the fretboard. The strongest notes again are the first (E), third (G) and fifth (B) forming the Em triad.

Like the Dorian mode, the Phrygian mode can be played over any form of the Em chord that adds a note from the scale: Em7 (add the dominant seventh (D)), Em6 (add the minor sixth (C)) and Em9 (add the ninth (F)) for example. The note added to the chord becomes a strong note. See the figure for the E Phrygian mode.

The Lydian mode of the C major scale starts on the fourth note (F). anywhere on the fretboard. Play pattern four starting on any F on the fretboard. The notes of the F Lydian mode are F, G, A, B, C, D, E and then start a new octave. The third note (A) is a major third so the Lydian mode is played over any form of F major chord, F, Fmaj7, F6 or F9. The strong notes are the first (F), third (A) and fifth (C) along with any note added to create a different form of the chord. See the figure for the F Lydian mode.

Starting with the fifth pattern on the fifth note of the C major scale (G) creates the Mixolydian mode. The Mixolydian mode is extremely popular in modern rock, country and pop music. The notes in the Mixolydian mode are G, A, B, C, D, E, F and back to G for the next octave. Since the third note (B) is a major third, the Mixolydian mode is played over a G major chord.

The seventh note is a flat seventh so the Mixolydian mode works with a G7 chord as opposed to the Gmaj7. The strong notes are the first (G), third (B), fifth (D) and seventh (F). The Mixolydian mode also works over different forms of the G major chord. See the figure for the G Mixolydian mode.

The Aeolian mode is created by playing pattern six starting on the sixth note of the C major scale (A) anywhere on the fretboard. The notes in the A Aeolian mode are A, B, C, D, E, F, G then starting a new octave at A. The strong notes are the first (A), third (C) and fifth (E) like all the other modes.

Since the third note is a minor third, the Aeolian mode is played over and Am chord as well as Am6 and Am9. Remember that if you play over a chord with an additional note, that note becomes a strong note in the scale. See the figure for the A Aeolian mode.

If play the seventh position on the seventh note (B) of the C major scale, you are playing the B Locrian mode. The notes for the B Locrian mode are B, C, D, E, F, G, A and back to B to start a new octave. While what can be considered strong notes are the first (B), third (D) and fifth (F), the Locrian mode is virtually useless. It sounds good over Bdimb5. See the figure for the B Locrian mode.

Looking at the figures for the C major scale, you will notice that all seven modes are using the same notes. What changes is the function of the notes. Songs in the key of C major use the following chords: C, Dm, Em, F, G, Am and Bdim. All of the information about the C major scale applies to the other scales only the notes change.

Summary of the Modes

All the information in the following section applies to all the keys. On the following pages I've included a chart showing the notes in each key as well as diagrams for the intervals in each mode or the keys.

Ionian mode – The natural major mode and is played over the major chord in all its forms for the given key. The intervals for the Ionian mode are: Root, major second, major third, perfect fourth, perfect fifth, major sixth and major seventh.

Dorian mode – It is played over the minor chord in all its forms for the second note in the key. The intervals for the Dorian mode are: Root, major second, flat third, perfect fourth, perfect fifth, major sixth and minor seventh.

Phrygian mode – it is played over the minor chord in all its forms for the third note in the key. The intervals for the Phrygian mode are: Root, flat second, flat third, perfect fourth, perfect fifth, flat sixth and flat seventh.

Lydian mode – it is played over the major chord in all its forms for the fourth note in the key. The intervals for the Lydian mode are: Root, major second, major third, sharp (augmented) fourth, perfect fifth, major sixth and major seventh.

Mixolydian mode – it is played over the major chord in all its forms for the fifth note in the key. The intervals for the Mixolydian mode are: Root, major second, major third, perfect fourth, perfect fifth, major sixth and minor seventh.

Aeolian mode – it is played over the minor chord in all its forms for the sixth note in the key. The intervals for the Aeolian mode are: Root, major second, minor third, perfect fourth, perfect fifth, minor sixth and major seventh.

Locrian mode – it is played over a diminished chord with a flat fifth for the seventh note. The intervals for the Locrian mode are: Root, minor second, minor third, perfect fourth, flat (diminished) fifth, minor sixth and minor seventh.

The following pages contain a chart and figures for all the keys. All the information about the C major key applies to the other keys only the notes change.

Mode	Interval						
	1	**2**	**3**	**4**	**5**	**6**	**7**
C Ionian	C	D	E	F	G	A	B
D Dorian	D	E	F	G	A	B	C
E Phrygian	E	F	G	A	B	C	D
F Lydian	F	G	A	B	C	D	E
G Mixolydian	G	A	B	C	D	E	F
A Aeolian	A	B	C	D	E	F	G
B Locrian	B	C	D	E	F	G	A

C Ionian

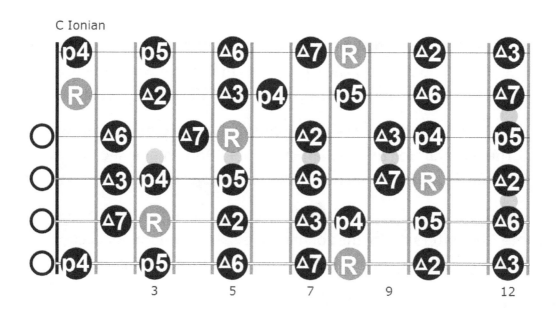

D Dorian

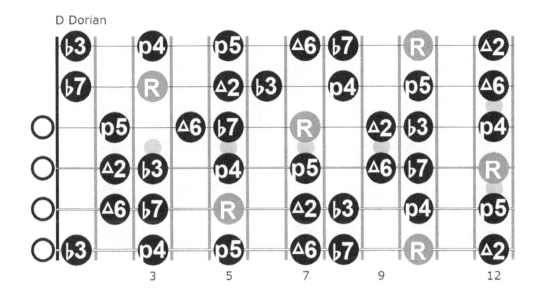

E Phrygian

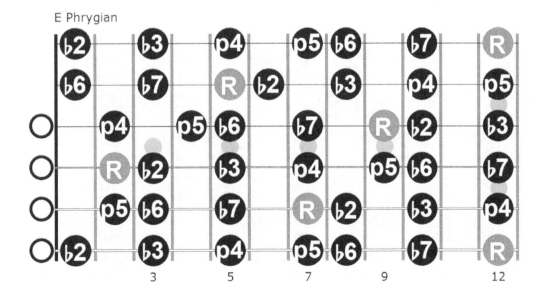

F Lydian

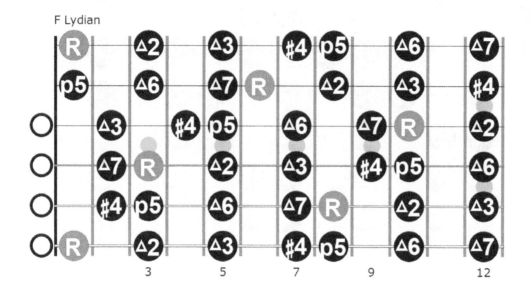

G Mixolydian

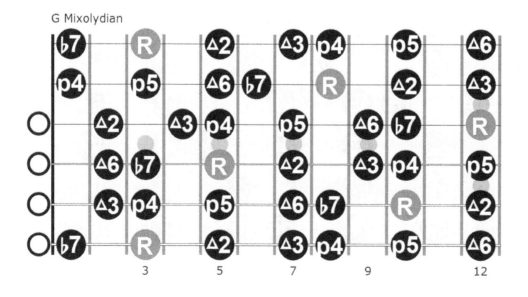

A Aeolian

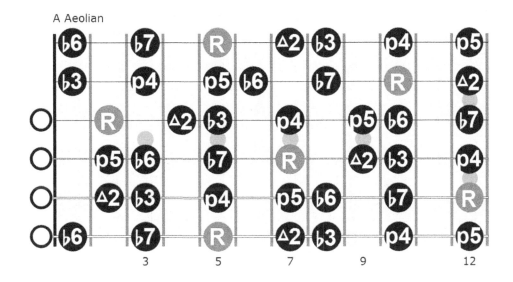

B Locian

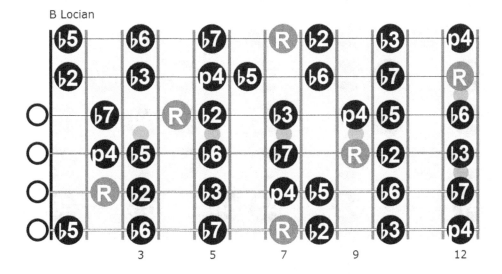

The G major Key

Mode	Interval						
	1	2	3	4	5	6	7
G Ionian	G	A	B	C	D	E	F#
A Dorian	A	B	C	D	E	F#	G
B Phrygian	B	C	D	E	F#	G	A
C Lydian	C	D	E	F#	G	A	B
D Mixolydian	D	E	F#	G	A	B	C
E Aeolian	E	F#	G	A	B	C	D
F# Locrian	F#	G	A	B	C	D	E

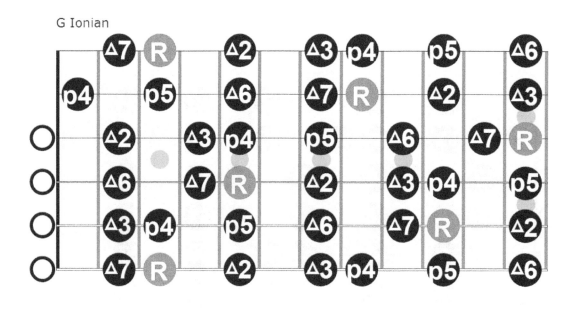

G Ionian

A Dorian

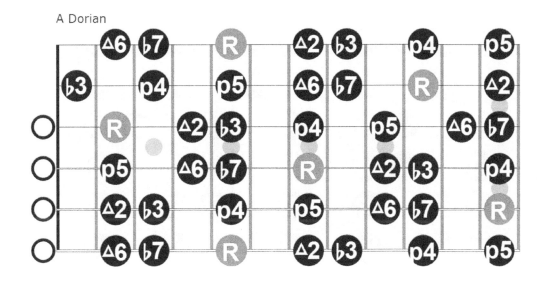

B Phrygian

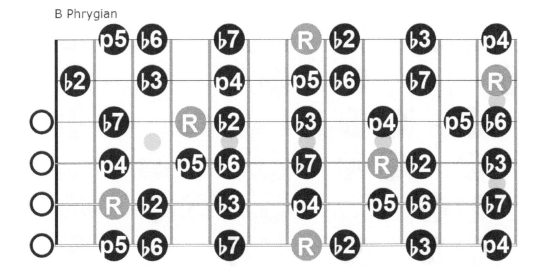

C Lydian

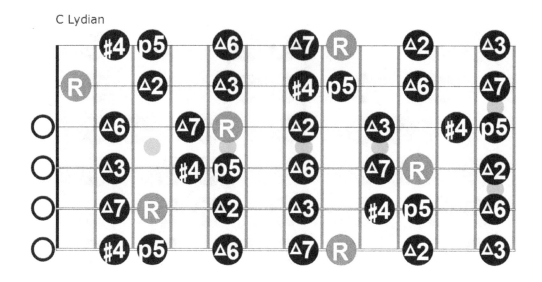

D Mixolydian

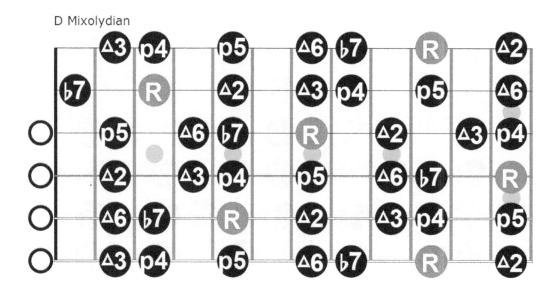

E Aeolian

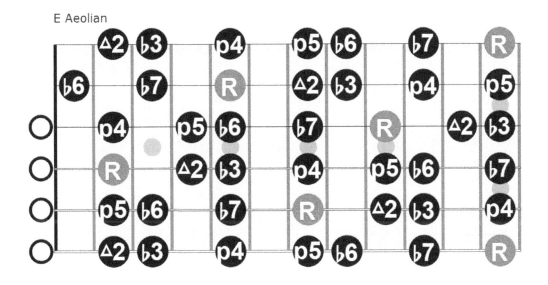

F# Locrian

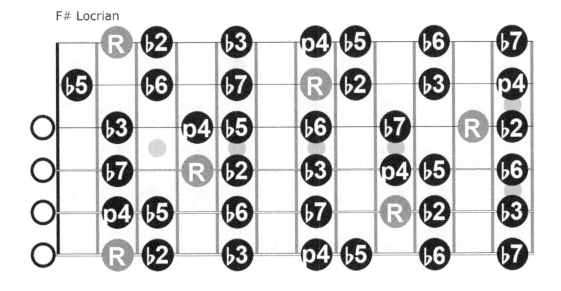

The D major Key

Mode	Interval						
	1	**2**	**3**	**4**	**5**	**6**	**7**
D Ionian	D	E	F#	G	A	B	C#
E Dorian	E	F#	G	A	B	C#	D
F# Phrygian	F#	G	A	B	C#	D	E
G Lydian	G	A	B	C#	D	E	F#
A Mixolydian	A	B	C#	D	E	F#	G
B Aeolian	B	C#	D	E	F#	G	A
C# Locrian	C#	D	E	F#	G	A	B

D Ionian

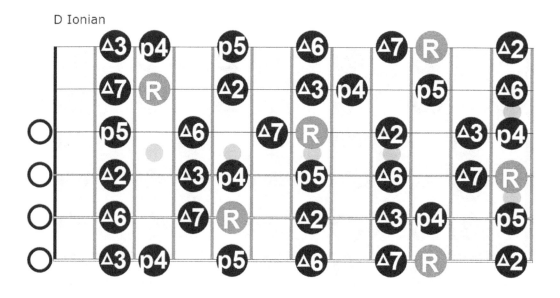

Mastering the Modes for Guitar

E Dorian

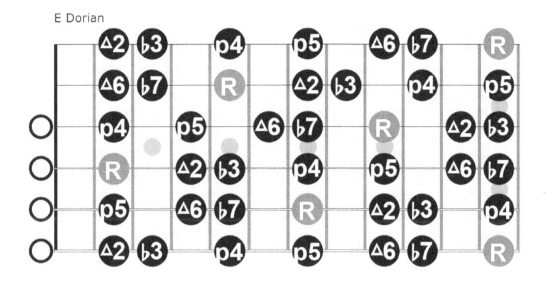

F# Phrygian

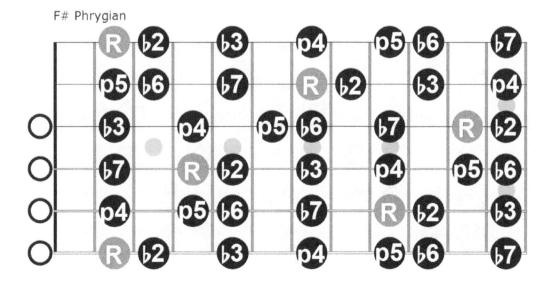

G Lydian

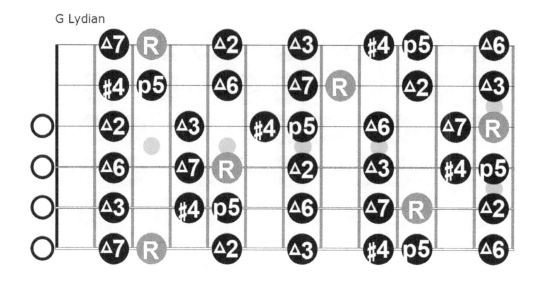

A Mixolydian

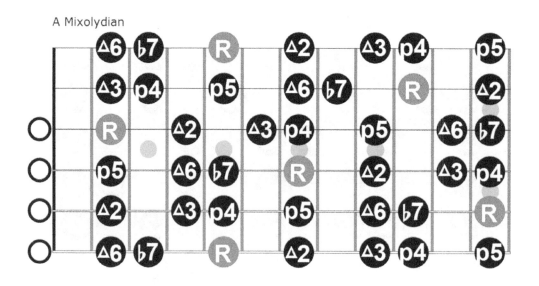

B Aeolian

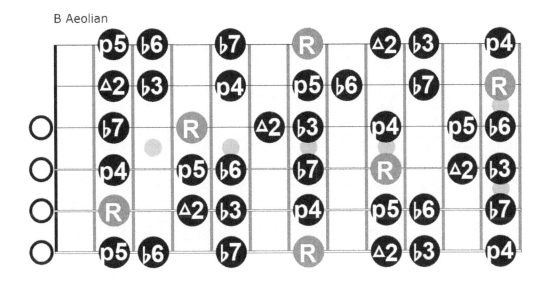

C# Locrian

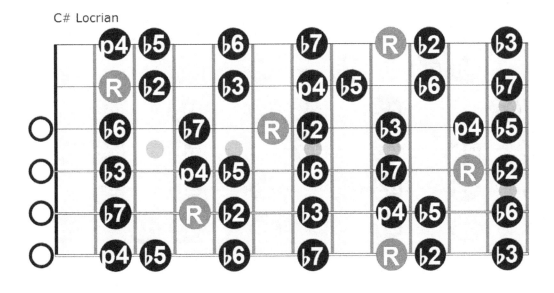

The A Major Key

Mode	Interval						
	1	2	3	4	5	6	7
A Ionian	A	B	C#	D	E	F#	G#
B Dorian	B	C#	D	E	F#	G#	A
C# Phrygian	C#	D	E	F#	G#	A	B
D Lydian	D	E	F#	G#	A	B	C#
E Mixolydian	E	F#	G#	A	B	C#	D
F# Aeolian	F#	G#	A	B	C#	D	E
G# Locrian	G#	A	B	C#	D	E	F#

A Ionian

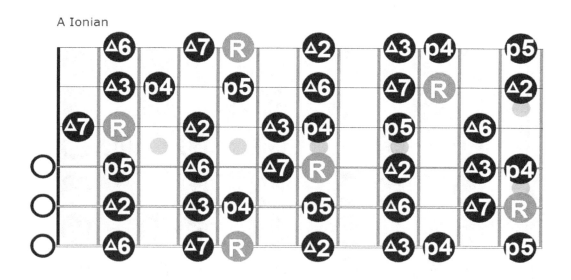

B Dorian

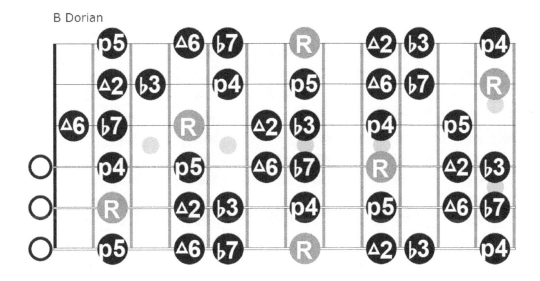

C# Phrygian

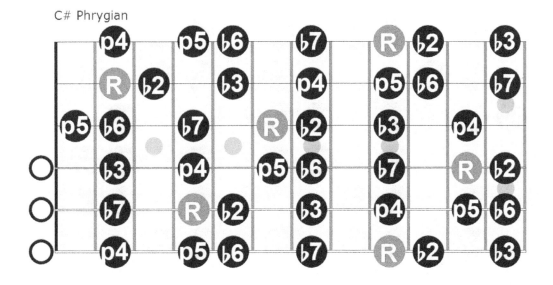

D Lydian

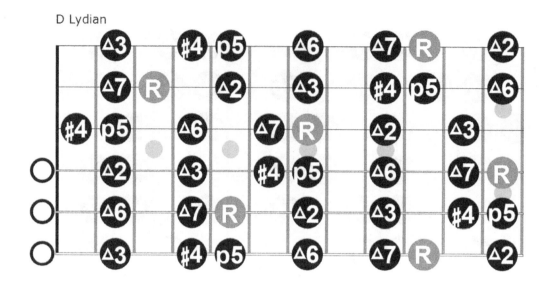

E Mixolydian

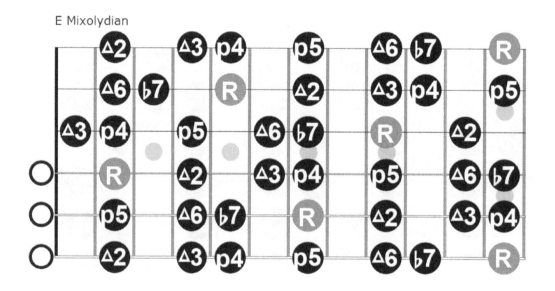

F# Aeolian

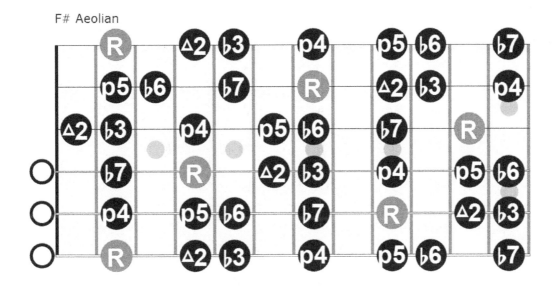

G# Locrian

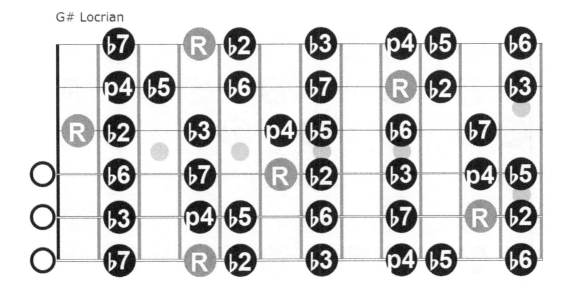

The E Major Key

Mode	Interval						
	1	2	3	4	5	6	7
E Ionian	E	F#	G#	A	B	C#	D#
F# Dorian	F#	G#	A	B	C#	D#	E
G# Phrygian	G#	A	B	C#	D#	E	F#
A Lydian	A	B	C#	D#	E	F#	G#
B Mixolydian	B	C#	D#	E	F#	G#	A
C# Aeolian	C#	D#	E	F#	G#	A	B
D# Locrian	D#	E	F#	G#	A	B	C#

E Ionian

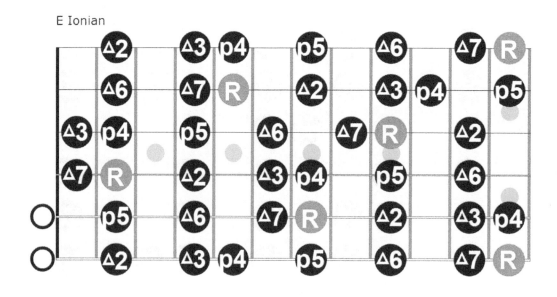

F# Dorian

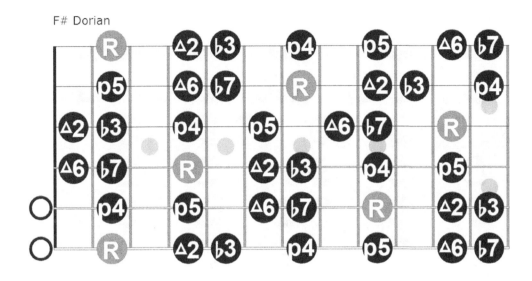

G# Phrygian

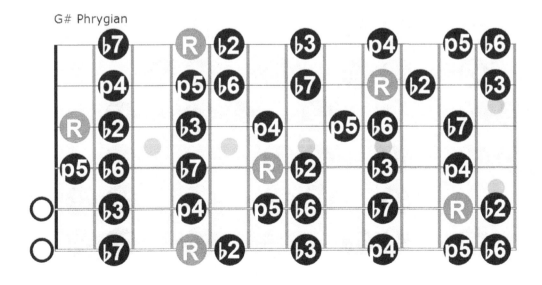

A Lydian

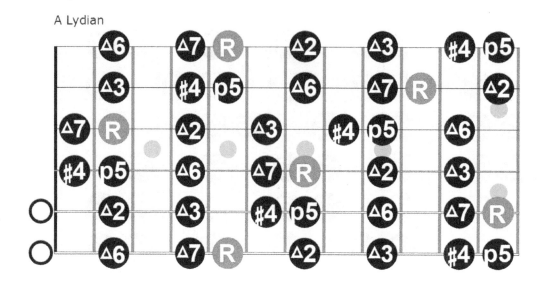

B Mixolydian

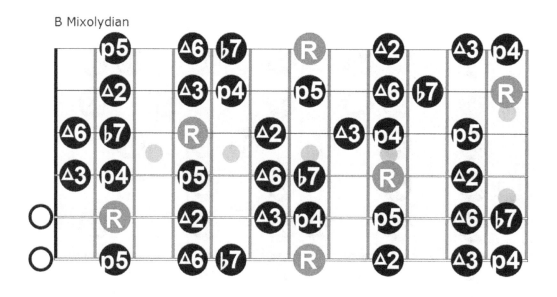

C# Aeolian

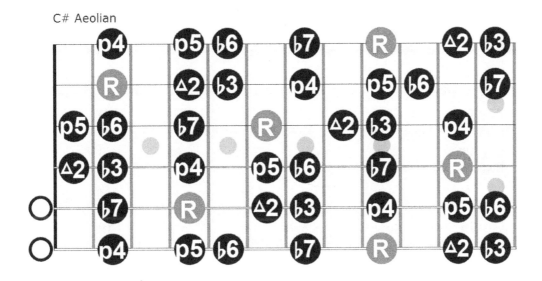

D# Locrian

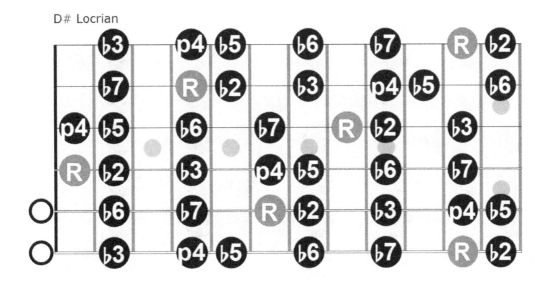

The B Major Key

Mode	Interval						
	1	2	3	4	5	6	7
B Ionian	B	C#	D#	E	F#	G#	A#
C# Dorian	C#	D#	E	F#	G#	A#	B
D# Phrygian	D#	E	F#	G#	A#	B	C#
E# Lydian	E	F#	G#	A#	B	C#	D#
F# Mixolydian	F#	G#	A#	B	C#	D#	E
G# Aeolian	G#	A#	B	C#	D#	E	F#
A Locrian	A#	B	C#	D#	E	F#	G#

B Ionian

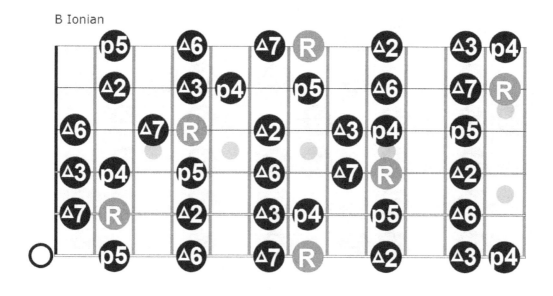

C# Dorian

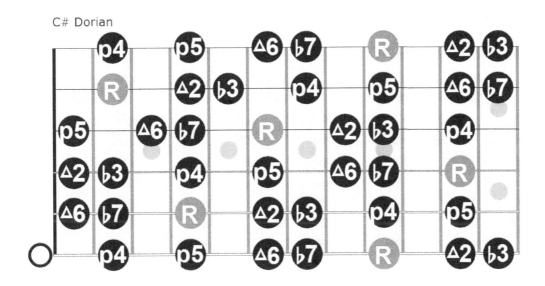

D# Phrygian

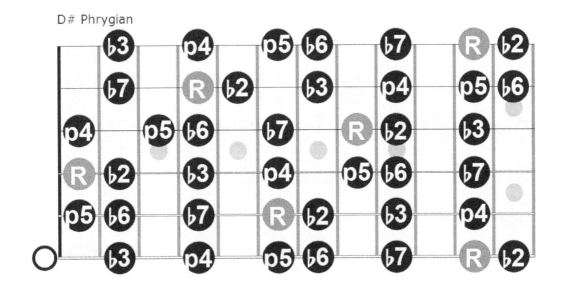

E Lydian

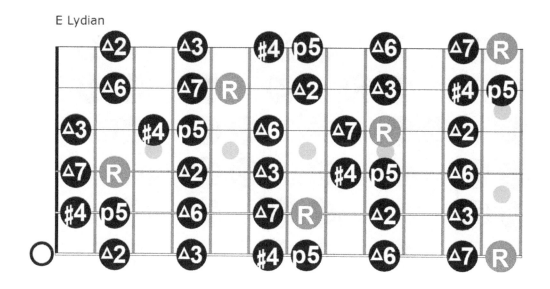

F# Mixolydian

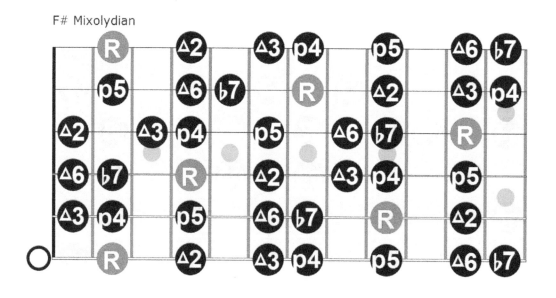

G# Aeolian

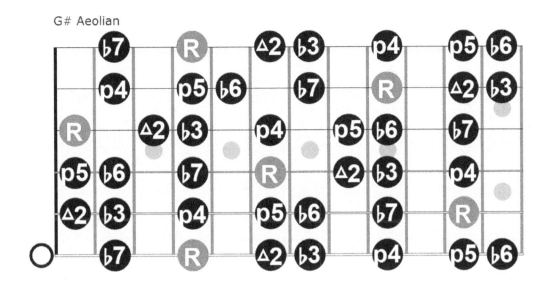

A# Locrian

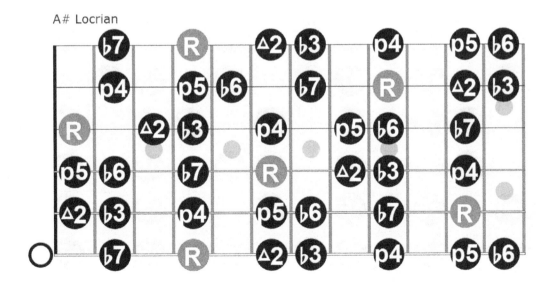

The F Major Key

Mode	Interval						
	1	2	3	4	5	6	7
F Ionian	F	G	A	Bb	C	D	E
G Dorian	G	A	Bb	C	D	E	F
A Phrygian	A	Bb	C	D	E	F	G
Bb Lydian	Bb	C	D	E	F	G	A
C Mixolydian	C	D	E	F	G	A	Bb
D Aeolian	D	E	F	G	A	Bb	C
E Locrian	E	F	G	A	Bb	C	D

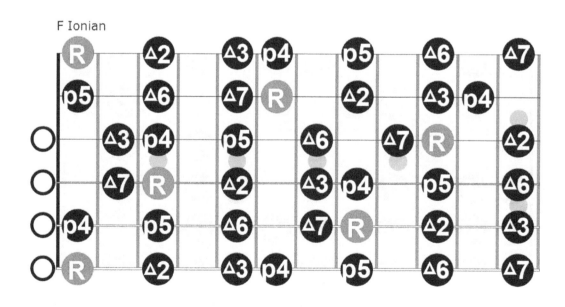

F Ionian

G Dorian

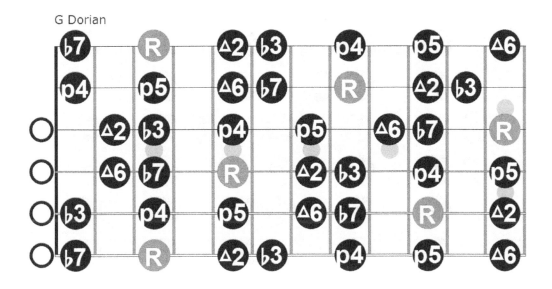

A Phrygian

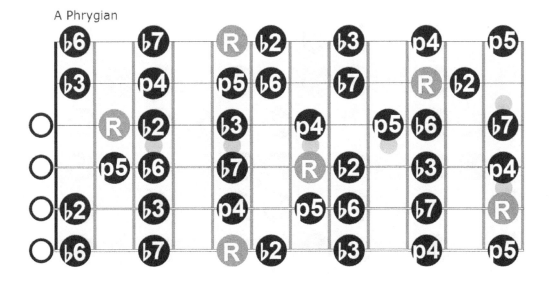

Bb Lydian

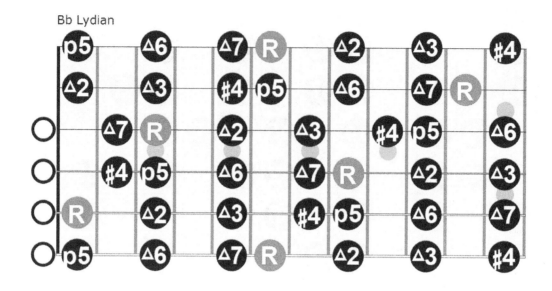

C Mixolydian

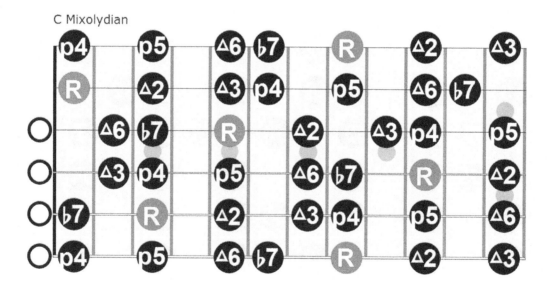

D Aeolian

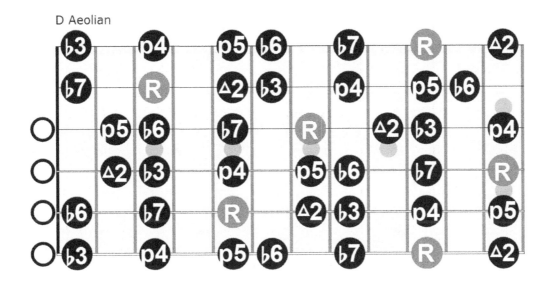

E Locrian

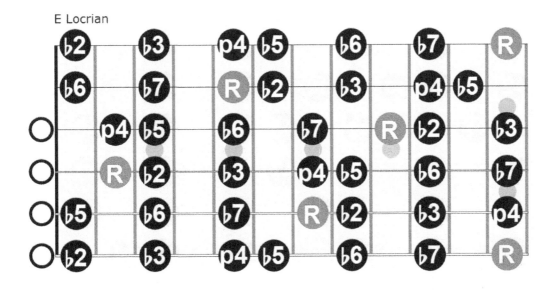

The Bb Major Key

Mode	Interval						
	1	2	3	4	5	6	7
Bb Ionian	Bb	C	D	Eb	F	G	A
C Dorian	C	D	Eb	F	G	A	Bb
D Phrygian	D	Eb	F	G	A	Bb	C
Eb Lydian	Eb	F	G	A	Bb	C	D
F Mixolydian	F	G	A	Bb	C	D	Eb
G Aeolian	G	A	Bb	C	D	Eb	F
A Locrian	A	Bb	C	D	Eb	F	G

Bb Ionian

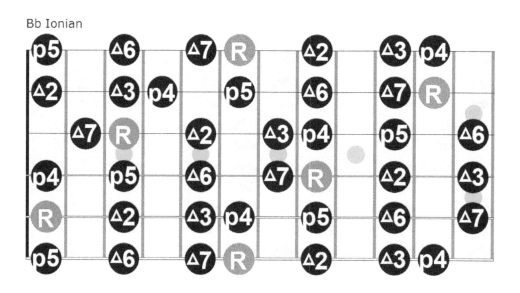

C Dorian

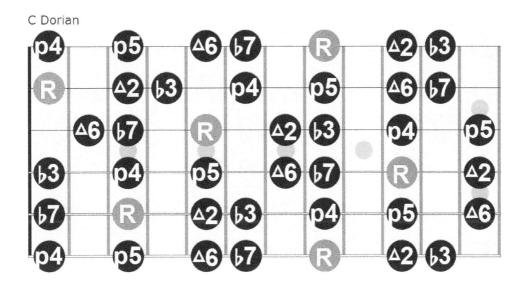

D Phrygian

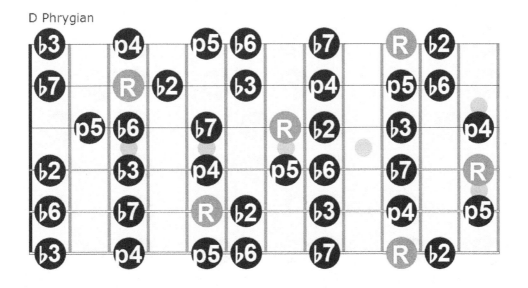

Eb Lydian

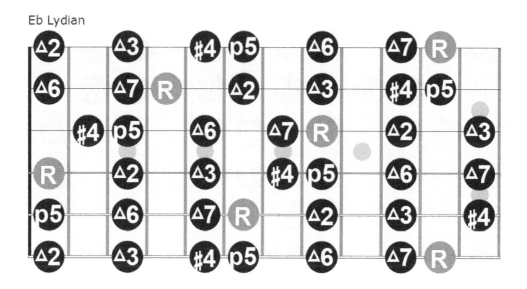

F Mixolydian

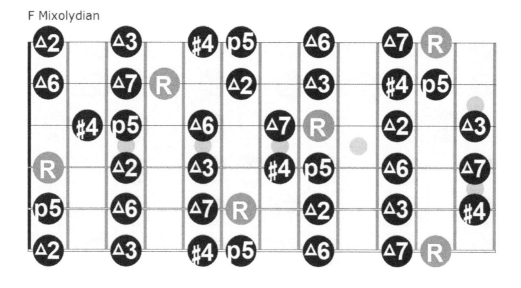

G Aeolian

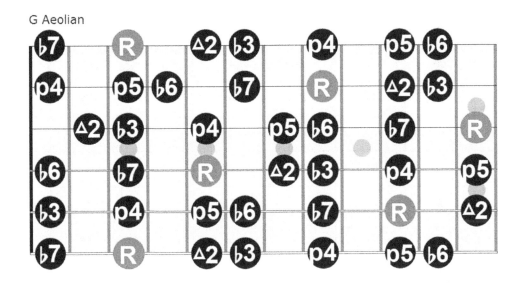

A Locrian

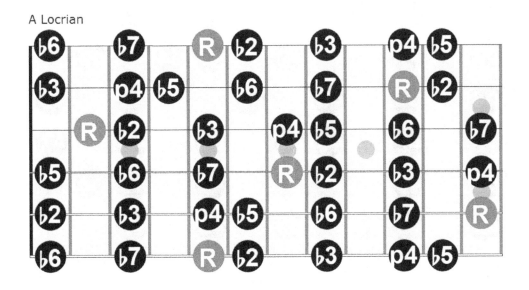

The Eb Major Key

Mode	Interval						
	1	2	3	4	5	6	7
Eb Ionian	Eb	F	G	Ab	Bb	C	D
F Dorian	F	G	Ab	Bb	C	D	Eb
G Phrygian	G	Ab	Bb	C	D	Eb	F
Ab Lydian	Ab	Bb	C	D	Eb	F	G
Bb Mixolydian	Bb	C	D	Eb	F	G	Ab
C Aeolian	C	D	Eb	F	G	Ab	Bb
D Locrian	D	Eb	F	G	Ab	Bb	C

Eb Ionian

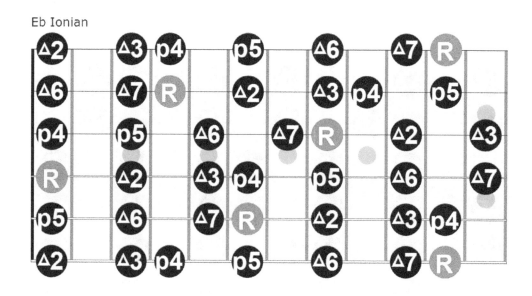

F Dorian

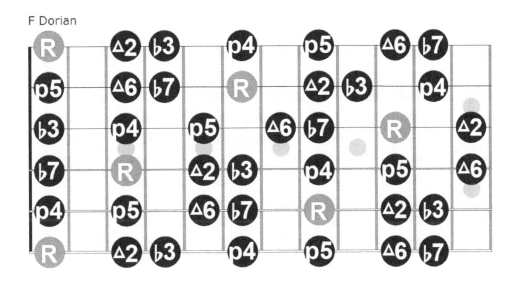

G Phrygian

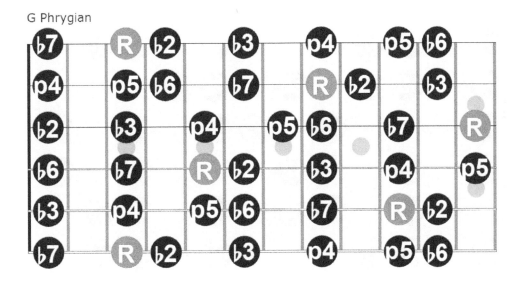

Ab Lydian

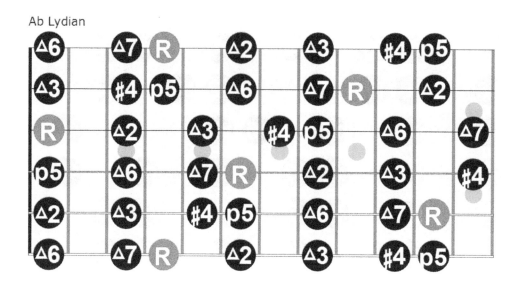

Bb Mixolydian

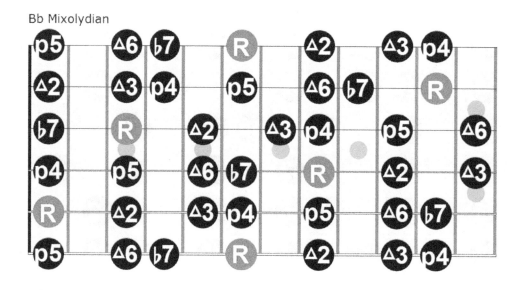

C Aeolian

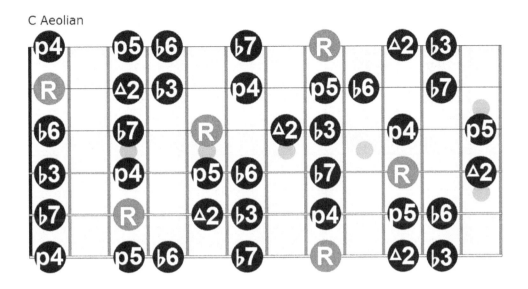

D Locrian

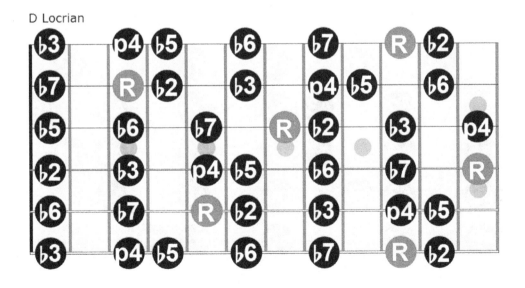

The Ab Major Key

Mode	Interval						
	1	**2**	**3**	**4**	**5**	**6**	**7**
Ab Ionian	Ab	Bb	C	Db	Eb	F	G
Bb Dorian	Bb	C	Db	Eb	F	G	Ab
C Phrygian	C	Db	Eb	F	G	Ab	Bb
Db Lydian	Db	Eb	F	G	Ab	Bb	C
Eb Mixolydian	Eb	F	G	Ab	Bb	C	Db
F Aeolian	F	G	Ab	Bb	C	Db	Eb
G Locrian	G	Ab	Bb	C	Db	Eb	F

Ab Ionian

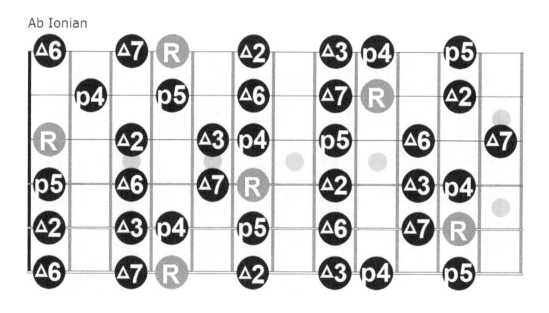

Bb Dorian

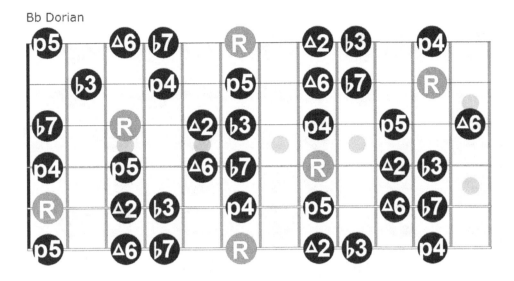

C Phrygian

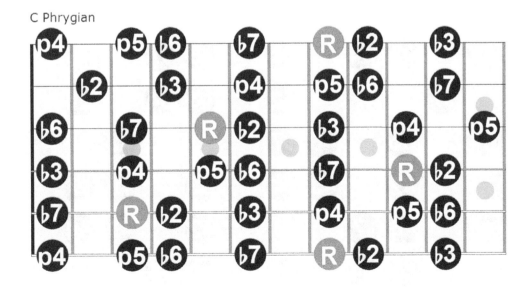

Db Lydian

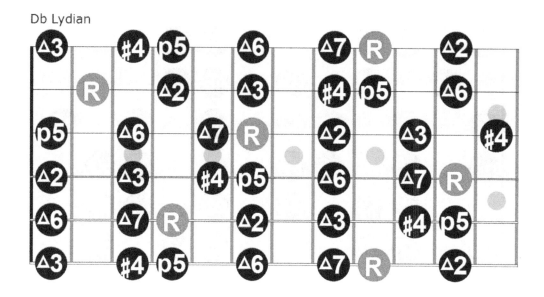

Eb Mixolydian

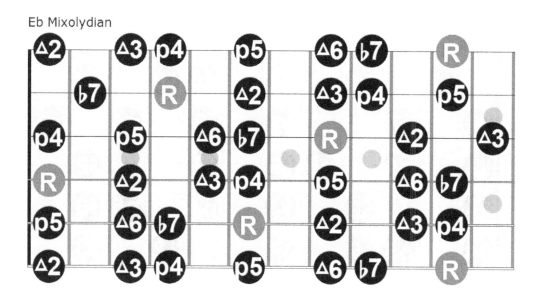

F Aeolian

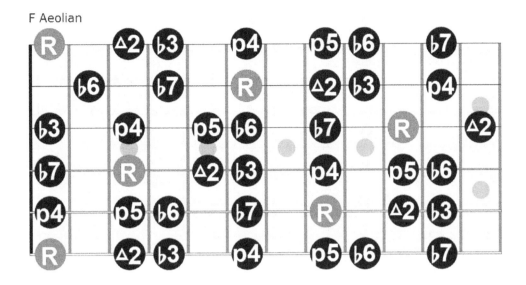

G Locrian

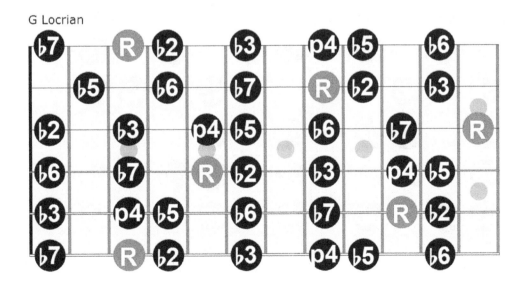

The Db Major Key

Mode	Interval						
	1	2	3	4	5	6	7
Db Ionian	Db	Eb	F	Gb	Ab	Bb	C
Eb Dorian	Eb	F	Gb	Ab	Bb	C	Db
F Phrygian	F	Gb	Ab	Bb	C	Db	Eb
Gb Lydian	Gb	Ab	Bb	C	Db	Eb	F
Ab Mixolydian	Ab	Bb	C	Db	Eb	F	Gb
Bb Aeolian	Bb	C	Db	Eb	F	Gb	Ab
C Locrian	C	Db	Eb	F	Gb	Ab	Bb

Db Ionian

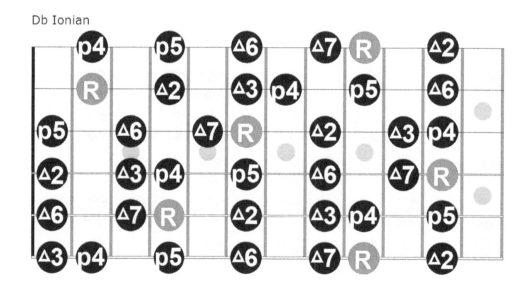

Eb Dorian

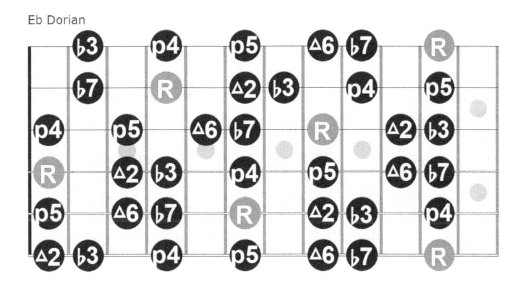

F Phrygian

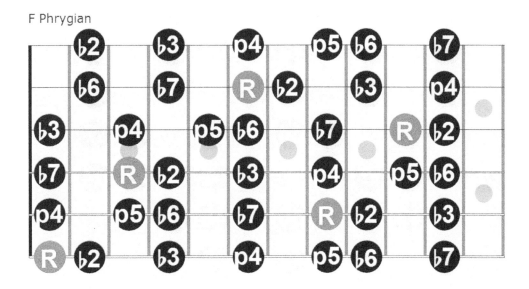

Gb Lydian

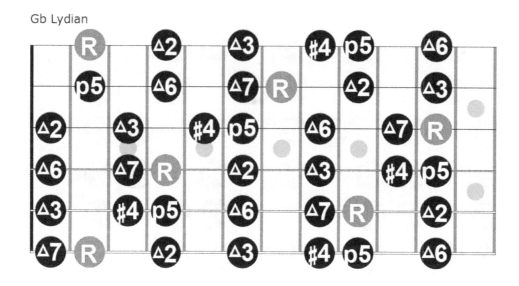

Ab Mixolydian

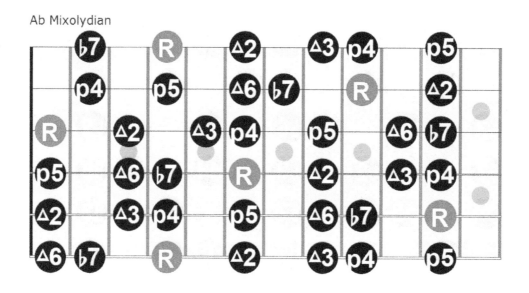

Bb Aeolian

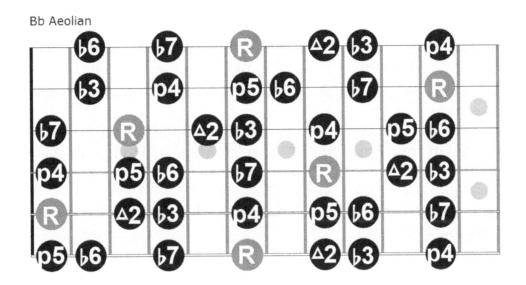

C Locrian

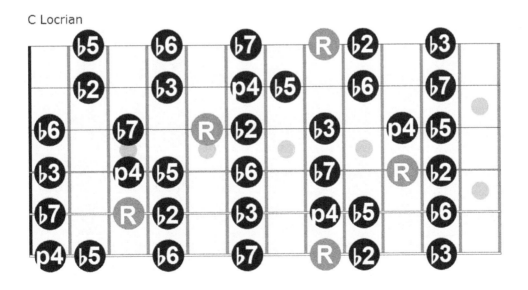

Afterwards

Thank you for reading my book. It is my sincere hope that you understand the major scales and their modes after finishing the book. If that is the case, please leave a review on Amazon.com. This helps me but more importantly it helps other guitarists looking for a better understanding of scales and modes.

I would like to thank my wonderful wife, Jo, for her support as well as my proof readers Darnell Butts and David Nesbit. They're support, and input have been invaluable.

A special thank you goes out to Jeanne Hansen for her work on some of the figures and the cover art.

A big thank you also goes out to Steve Stine for writing the forward for this book. In my opinion, Steve is the best guitar instructor on the web. His lessons can be found at guitarzoom.com.

You can check out some of my music on at:
https://www.reverbnation.com/glenross

Made in United States
Orlando, FL
14 March 2024

44668612R00052